Cultural M

A Practical Guide to Multi...

C000143526

sketches, texts, and stories by

FRANK DAVEY

Talonbooks • Vancouver • 1996

TALONBOOKS
104 — 3100 Production Way
Burnaby, British Columbia V5A 4R4
Canada

Published with assistance from the Canada Council

Printed and bound in Canada by Hignell Printing Limited

CANADIAN CATALOGUING IN PUBLICATION DATA
Davey, Frank, 1940 -
Cultural mischief
ISBN 0-88922-364-5
1. Multiculturalism — Canada —Literary collections.
2. Pluralism (Social sciences) — Canada.
3. Multiculturalism — Literary collections.
4. Pluralism (Social sciences) — Literary collections.
I. Title.
PS 8557.A63C84 1996   C818'.5408   C96-910076-0
PR9199.3.D28C84 1966

Contents

My Brown Dog

My Brown Dog

My brown dog is not a brown dog but a fawn dog with black stripes.

My brown dog's mother was a fawn dog but his father was not a black dog or a brown dog but a fawn dog with black stripes.

My brown dog would be happy to mate with a black dog. Or a blue dog or a green dog.

Discrimination requires culture and culture requires high levels of consciousness.

My brown dog is always conscious of other dogs.

Domestication of dogs marked one of those dawns of culture.

At 160 lbs, with good hips, deep chest, scissors bite, newly brushed coat, my brown dog struts like a brown dog.

My brown dog yearns rarely for the land of his ancestors.

My brown dog would mate with a small dog if he could figure out the vectors and trajectories necessary. But if he could figure out vectors and trajectories he would have a higher level of consciousness.

My brown dog bounds indiscriminately whenever he meets a big, little, brown, black, or otherwise configured dog. Indiscriminately here also means promiscuously.

Willingness to mate is the highest compliment my dog can offer, although he will also substitute willingness to play or willingness to ignore.

Culture means having a promiscuous but not indiscriminate intelligence.

Culture has brought us infinite numbers of substitutions for willingness to mate, many of these unconscious.

My brown dog can get along with any other male dog once he knows who can beat the shit out of whom. This he understands as the dog-pack social model. Here dog culture is only slightly behind human culture.

Culture has advantages and disadvantages.

My brown dog has been called a *dogue allemand* but very few hold that against him.

My brown dog has been called a *grand danois,* which in France suggests cinnamon or cherries.

My brown dog would bark several times to assist his brother dog, who is a fawn dog, or to help his human of whatever colour, size, class, citzenship, or imagined gender.

Although excluded from food stores, restaurants, and some hotels, my brown dog because of his dog-pack social model imagines few center-margin conflicts.

My brown dog will run on a brown leash a red leash or a white leash. He would run on a black leash but I don't have a black leash.

People also run on leashes and some of those leashes have been called culture.

A good dog can hold its own leash.

My brown dog often hears that he is a good dog but humans hear only rarely that they are good people.

10

Good Bomb

Most bombs today are made from the left. This is because the new global economy gives fascists everywhere improved access to power.

Most bombs today are made from the right. Fertilizer and fuel oil assert pastoral lives threatened by the new global economy.

Bombs announce what a bomber values. The Italian Mafia bomb the Uffizi. Hamas bombs a cultural centre, a bus, a shopping mall. Certain Bosnians bomb schoolyards and marketplaces. Chechens bomb tanks. Algerians bomb the Champs Elysées. Russians bomb milk cows.

The Unabomber bombs technophiles with technically subtle bombs.

The gregarious Irish bomb.

Some people make bombs, or poems, or stories about bombs, for fun. This can be a subtle sign of power.

The Most Famous Canadian Bombmaker is Albert Guay who in 1947 blew up 26 people in an airliner so he could collect his wife's insurance. English-Canadians would love to be able to remember Albert Guay.

Carbombs can be personal or public. This distinction can become a problem in teleology.

Lionel Kearns has theorized poems that detone. They too would be a kind of power.

Rajiv Gandhi's bomb came in a disarming package.

The Most Famous Canadian Bombmaker is Joseph Chartier whose bomb blew up when he stopped for a leak in a washroom of the House of Commons. English-Canadians would giggle if they could remember Joseph Chartier.

Most people wish the briefcase bomb planted next to Adolph Hitler had succeeded. Most people wish otherwise of the bomb planted in Oklahoma City. Most people means me and probably you. Planted means nostalgia for corn-roasts and barn dances.

Few Canadians remember the blond Vancouver kids who bombed the windows out of Litton Systems. Few Canadians means me and once in a while you.

Klein blasts Parizeau.

Official bombs, bombs paraded under flags down sunny boulevards, are unsubtle signs of power.

We stopped in a Champs Elysées cafe one morning and that afternoon a Hamadi brothers bomb wrecked it. Most bombs illuminate both cultural and space-time issues.

Official bombs are built on assembly lines along with pressure cookers, microwaves, and TV sets.

Bouchard blasts Manning.

The Most Famous Canadian Bombmaker is that guy what's his name, in the yellow turban, whose bomb blew up the Air India jumbo.

As a kid, I used to enjoy lighting and throwing hundreds of firecrackers each Hallowe'en. Enjoy means get a bang out of, have a blast.

Pipe bombs can be made by filling a piece of galvanized pipe with matchheads. Some law-abiding Canadians hope the bombmaker tamps the matchheads sharply.

Sneaky bombs—bombs in lunch boxes, briefcases, radios, mail boxes, women's blouses, rented trucks, Hells Angels' jeeps—can be a sign of not-enough power.

The irresistible power of a bomb headline.

A suicide bomb is a primitive smart bomb.

A clever carbomb integrates the victim into its detonator.

Clever bombs surround you and me with implied bombs: the x-ray machine at the airport, the truck overparked on your sidestreet, the missing lockers at the train station.

Powerboat explodes mysteriously near Port Stanley.

Some bombs, like the one that destroyed the King David Hotel, launch political careers. This can be called good or bad bombing.

Bombs create perspective.

Some bombs, like the one that destroyed the U.S. Marine Barracks in Beirut, end political careers. This too can be called good or bad bombing.

A political minefield.

Two of my high-school friends used to build pipe-bombs and explode them in an empty pasture.

Yet bombmaking tales are incomplete, are fragmentary, are duds without the big bomb, the Bomb, the Bomb that each year in a thousand speeches keeps millions of nice young Japanese and American boys from fighting and dying, and people everywhere from fighting wars and bombing.

Good bomb thus means not just the one you or your friends drop, throw, set, plant, or otherwise detone. Good bomb means the one that bursts right before bunches of people get new understandings, rules, limbs, pride, multicultural agreements, a good time, families, lots of money, lower tariffs, a new country, well-made VCRs, and forget all about us others happily making good bombs.

16

Narcissus Copies

1.

Narcissus Copies: a sign, a shop on Bloor Street West. People infatuated with their own writing come from miles around. The copy looks deeper and richer than the original. The shop uses only the whitest of papers. Author of best-selling novel now can hold head high. Many customers demand multiple copies. More than five billion certified. Next door is an essay service stocked with the work of three generations of outstanding students.

2.

Narcissus copies Narcissus copies. Great authors write the same book over and over. Repeaters always prosper. You can find similar copy shops within blocks of almost every university campus. New franchising rules let everybody win. Pressured by professional artists, government tables stringent new legislation on quotation and duplication. A true original. Just one great poem after another. Computer generated information. Text transfer. On-line graphics. Camera-ready copy. Renewable resources. Multiple listings. A good copying service will obtain all necessary permissions from yourself within 24 hours.

3.

Monkeys attack Indian government office and shred key files. Police watch helplessly. The forty-three monkeys arrived just after coffeebreak on Tuesday morning. Mr. Charan Tappar was seated at his desk inscribing marriage data when the first animal leapt through his open window from its perch beneath the eaves. Monkeys are considered sacred and wise by most devout Hindus. Mr. Tappar immediately alerted his colleagues by calling 'Monkey-ji, monkey-ji,' or something like this in Hindi. Many of the files were severely bitten and masticated. He and his colleagues fled the ensuing invasion in bafflement. To attack a monkey is to attack a human soul. Or a version of a human soul. Mr. Tappar and Mr. Kesari, his director, lamented the office's lack of copying facilities. After 25 minutes, discouraged by the frequent paperclips and staples, the monkeys angrily returned to their homes in the building's attic.

4.

As for her, she can download legislation to her home terminal in less than seven keystrokes. The current laser printer standard is 12 pages per minute. I have a friend who designs, typesets and prints all his own books, and then prices them high enough that he can keep every copy. Repeaters ring the quarter-hours. More books by Mordecai Richler sell internationally than by any other Canadian literary author. I have another friend who has bought a special bookcase for the issues of periodicals in which he is published. You can learn more by copying someone else's writing than by copying your own.

5.

Narcissus copies and copies. Businesses on the main streets near universities are protected from recessions. Everybody thinks I steal sentences from books and newspapers. Trisha Romance prints. The coffee looks richer and deeper than the original. Although you may see all kinds of folk dive right in, nothing you read is necessarily true, even if you've just written it. People, mostly students, rush in and out of the place anyway. No one can enter the same facts twice. No one can enter the same fax twice.

6.

Montreal critic plagued by misspelling. Words have their own meanings, offended publisher announces, insisting he is not the missing professor Lacker. No copy quite like its original. Lack of proofreading, professor complains, has again produced a Norbert Pecker. Canlit reified as Montreal publisher reprints new series. No time like the presence. Search resumed for Professor Hecker. Four more articles by Rupert Backer. In his new book Dr. Licker argues once more that CanLit ordered by cosmic harmony. Comic harmony. Cosmic hominy. Comic homily. No time like press time. Cross-country alert re-issued for Professor Flacker. Gritty performance, sports pundits declare, by Professor Becker. No rest for the written. Dogged by misspellings, Professor Recker issues new copies of his much cited disclaimer. All-out hunt for Professor Drecker.

7.

Perlette, a Chapman zebra, was born Saturday at the Amneville zoo. Despite being born in captivity, Perlette has all the regular characteristics and markings of a Chapman zebra. This birth, the first zoo-birth of a female Chapman zebra in three or four years, comes only weeks after the birth of a killer whale at a Canadian aquarium. Perlette's mother delivered in a heated litter specially designed for the circumstance. The sixth Marseille hotel robbery of the holiday season followed the pattern of the others. The robbers struck just after midnight and, after threatening to waken and rob the guests, were given access to the hotel safe. Another baby killer whale dies at Canadian aquarium.

8.

In the evening the river seems to run more slowly and the willow trees above its banks to cease their sighing. It makes you proud to be an author. A very few customers have been worried that their texts might be reversed. While the photo-copiers of the nation continue turning. Some theorists have invoked metaphors of reproduction, machines that go bang in the night, prolific authors, promiscuous textualities.

9.

Calgary-born writer, Paris writer, Canadian exile, wins prix du Gouverneur général. 'Qui a peur de Nancy Huston?' I quote this original remark from *Le Devoir* without translating. Expat Prairie writer steals prize for French copy of her first English-Canadian novel. For her fourth novel in French. For a second original version. For a selftranslation. For an account already accounted. A tale already told. I translate this from the French of Jacques Allard. French copy of Canadian writer wins French-Canadian prize. 'Qui a peur de Francy Huston?' I quote myself without translating. French copy of English-Canadian novel defeats thirty-three French-language originals. First follows second. First humiliated by second. 'Albertaine-Parisienne-anglophone-francophone' lifts most sought-after prize. I translate freely.

10.

Ooooooh, says the pigeon, over and over. Art in the age of mechanical reproduction is like the child in the carseat endlessly rocking. New safety questions about the Meme implant. One major problem with quotation is that it requires an audience that reads more than its own writing. One cause of dwindling literary markets. I try to steal mostly from writers who might read my writing. She said. Meanwhile volcanos proliferate all around the Pacific rim, repeated outpourings of joy. Narcissi, Narcissi! Move very quickly whenever you repeat yourself.

11.

Pigeons threaten to overwhelm Canadian writer's home. Hundreds of pigeons reported nesting in the eaves of Ottawa writer John Metcalf. Does paper re-cycling endanger the nation's archives? Beleaguered family hurls mothballs at complacent pigeons. Each morning, witnesses report, the layer of guano on the sills and and gutters of the building increases, seriously threatening its structural integrity. Can blue box programs survive? Novelist reports that fellow writer's attempt to control pigeon outbreak with poisoned corn has resulted in deaths of 15 pigeons, 7 songbirds, and her neighbour's cat. New standards for processed effluent. Smell of pigeons and smell of death influencing his writing, desperate English novelist alleges.

12.

Considered semantically, to repeat is not the same as to regurgitate. A creature of a different stripe. Spit it out says the dentist, the policeman, the mother. Many birds. The evil of the foreign object. You could tell when he read aloud that he loved the sound of words, of his words, of a rich voice speaking those words. Every three years, a new constitutional conference. So I repeat myself, he said, I speak for multitudes. A typical Ottawa writer. French narcs are called *stups.* Up and down the street, the great Narcissus keeps busy. No ocular malice for this guy. A closed circuit of production—safe sex, private inspiration. You too can save your country from the disgrace of compromise, AND rescue literature from the infinite play of signification.

Masculinist Mischief

Masculinist Mischief

(for John Fekete)

1.

First-place in the purchase of underpants is held by English-women, who on average purchase 7 per year. Right behind are Spanish women who purchase 6.2 pairs and German who purchase 4.8. In the rear, at the bottom, at the tail-end are phrases to be avoided. Last, that is, are Italian women who buy only 3 per year, and no more than one brassiere. All this is apparently true, and published le 27 decembre, 1992. Some retail observers speculate about differences in diet or climate. Others look for correlations with cosmetics, perfumes or cosmetic surgery, or attempt complex analyses of national variations in female self-image.

2.

Here in Toronto statistics on underwear sales to men are currently unavailable. This lack is unfortunate both politically and poetically. *A Little Night Magic* continues at Harper's Dinner Theatre. Men's briefs come in four basic models and in a more limited range of colours. Theatre Passe-Muraille presents *The Tyrant of Pontus.* Despite radically different market conditions, much interest continues in third-world figures. Listen, sweetie, I heard this on 'Business Magazine.' Men can be divided between those who wear undershirts the year round and those for whom they are at best winter clothing. The Scarborough Village Theatre—some seats still available for *Agnes of God.* Brief design has been strongly influenced by the evolution of the athletic support. Jan. 17 - Feb. 8 at Village Playhouse: *Sinners* by Norm Foster.

3.

During 1968-1974, the first period of activist feminism, lingerie, previously the chief medium of feminine eroticism, fell into disrepute, many women discarding the brassiere altogether. Annie wanted to know who says. In the late 1970s triumphantly reborn femininity overthrew the old boundaries between undergarments and clothing. A young reporter for the *Nice-Matin.* Eager couturiers re-invented the crinoline, the wasp-waisted corset and the garter-belt, ushering in a period of intense interchange: undergarments could replace the negligee or traditional elements of outer clothing, while the latter could be worn next to the body itself. I told her it was my own loose-fitting translation. The erotic mystery of lingerie became the mystery of what might underlie the visible.

4.

On the big night every eye in the hall turned to catch the entry of the baddest girl of all. I will be so relieved dearest, as relieved as I know you will be, when all this is over. Ten pounds of sugar, imagine, ten pounds of sugar. The feminist challenge in art—if one can be nailed down at all—replaces the monumental and exotic with the intimate and domestic. You remember falsies? Alarmed by his mother's new attempt on his life, the prince fled to the mountains and was for many years a hunter. Guelph co-ed convicted after topless protest romp. New medical concerns. Protect yourself, men lie. The free woman, of course, achieves climax without sacrificing her freedom and integrity. Even though I knew it would make you unhappy. 2 cups flour, 1/2 cup brown sugar, 8 eggs, 2 lb. raisins, 1/2 tbsp. allspice, 1 lb. currents, 1 lb. mixed peel, 1/4 lb. ground almonds, brandy. All proceeds go. In the beginning *mischief* meant calamity, real big trouble.

5.

It was her great-grandmother's recipe. Amid the renewed activism of the 1980s women became less concerned with visible display. In 1990 only 200 million bras were sold in all of Western Europe, with most carefully designed (de-signed, she explained) to follow and enhance natural human contours. English women were also far in front (in front?) in the purchase of this item, with an annual rate of 1.8. They were followed by French women at 1.4, the Spanish at 1.3 and the Germans at 1.2. Many of those intimate with the industry regard the small size of the Italian market as a mystery. I am just translating what I read. Despite widespread interest, statistics on colour, size and style variations between countries have to date not been made public. American sales of the Wonderbra swell dramatically. Textual producers everywhere strive to profit from social customs.

Female Circumcision

Is practiced mainly by blacks and so is arguably a matter only blacks should argue.

Is practiced mainly by Somali and Ethopian blacks and so is arguably only a matter Somali and Ethiopian blacks should argue.

Is practiced mainly in the name of marriage and so is arguably a matter only married people should argue.

Will never happen to me or my dog and so neither should argue.

Is practiced despite the inaccuracy of the word 'circumcision.'

Is practiced in western culture mainly by rapists and sex

slayers.

Is practiced in western culture mainly by displacement, metaphor, and sublimation.

Is practiced as an example of cultural practice.

Is practiced in cultures that insist on their right to their own cultures.

Is practiced alongside bride burning, foot binding, face veiling, ear and nose piercing, infant gender selecting, lip painting, female infanticide, dieting, breast implanting, unemploying, underpaying.

Globalized Sex

1.

My white friend Renny said it might be real neat to breed with a black girl. He had been reading Laferrière's Québec classic *How to Make Love to a Negro.*

My Alberta cousin who fought in the Korean War came back with a beautiful Japanese wife. A lot better than he could have done here, my dad said.

Rajiv Gandhi's Italian wife was never a political liability.

Japanese men fly by the thousands to visit Thailand.

Small gifts can forge ties between large and small countries.

When he was thirteen, my friend Larry and his sister gave

free sex demos to their Mennonite and non-Mennonite classmates.

The nigger-in-the-woodpile is a concept produced by economic relations.

My great-uncle lived with a young Chinese woman for almost a decade and after was said to have been a lot more good-humoured than he had been earlier.

My friend Rob said that someday we would all be the same colour and he wanted to be on the leading edge.

Lynch mobs are normally male and uni-racial.

The quickening speed of international travel.

My dad would whistle under his breath at white, Sikh, or Chinese young women. I believed he was shy.

An other-race lover has a higher status among liberal than among conservative intellectuals.

Who are more evil?—the Nazis who enjoyed sex with the Jews they were about to kill or the Nazis who thought such sex disgusting?

Comment faire l'amour avec un nègre became a Québécois bestseller because of its amusing portrayal of white anglophone women.

Pocahontas is remembered because she met a certain John Smith.

One of my dad's favorite kinds of reading was short pulp fiction about half-naked Nazi vamps with whips and jack-boots. I imagined he imagined saving them.

In the present economy most inquiries into hybridized sexuality still focus on women.

Pauline Johnson really did title her first book *White Wampum.*

Beware of Catholic girls, advised my mother.

Evelyn Lau writes that she had mainly, but not entirely, white customers.

In a small widely-scattered society, the Inuit practice of welcoming a visitor to the bed of a wife or daughter had genetic as well as social advantages.

A catalogue of Russian brides.

My dad worked to have the 'Caucasian' restriction removed from his Eagles lodge.

Some genes are more fashionable, i.e. tradeable, than other genes.

Lucien Bouchard called for more white québécois-speaking

babies.

Comment faire l'amour avec un nègre became a Quebec bestseller because of needs created by the new global economy.

Women have been more selective than men because their prosperity has been more often tied to the prosperity of their children.

The status of the other-race lover can depend on international money traders.

Catholic girls, warned my mother, do it on purpose to snare Protestant boys.

Most French and Scottish traders had no difficulty finding wives in Rupert's Land.

Most white women have no difficulty finding lovers in India.

Women have been more selective than men because in most cultures men have preferred more or less selective women.

Beware of Tamil women bearing gifts.

Mixed marriages helped establish and topple Apartheid.

John Smith, early global economist, is remembered.

Catholic girls, said my mother, are under orders from the Church.

Small gifts can forge ties between large and small institutions.

Does anyone else remember Pierre Sevigny and Gerda Munsinger?

Over the decades, in the service of universal peace and prosperity, I and other Canadian boys have ourselves undertaken to sexually fantasize Princess Margaret, Dorothy of Oz,

Anne Frank, Eartha Kitt, Florence Nightingale, Cecile Dion, Joan Baez, Kahntineta Horn, Jane Fonda, Emma Goldman, Shirley Yamaguchi, Heidi Eichmann, Princess Anastasia, Shirley Temple Black, Camille Claudel, Barbara Ann Scott, Besamir Bhutto.

Many of us would have gladly extended this heterosexual text but for AIDS and the chronic global shortfall in imaginable partners.

Cultural Mischief

My Yugoslav Friends

My Yugoslav friends are now my Serbian, Croatian, Macedonian, Slovenian, and Bosnian friends.

My Serb friend Dusko weeps on the phone from Belgrade because he's heard that Serb children are being murdered near Sarajevo.

My Croat friend Branko sighs because even the trees have been shot and left to die on the farms south of Zagreb.

My Slovene friend Igor recalls the quiet cobblestones of Dubrovnik.

My Serb friend Mitrovic, the not-so-secret security agent, told my wife I was poet and had soul of a Slav.

My Bosnian friend Abdullah has disappeared only days after

witnessing three young men being murdered in Mostar.

My Krajina friend Ljiljana says that her parents are now refugees in Serbia, and that Croat soldiers are living in her family home.

My Bosnian friend Bogdan urged me, October 1991, to drive down to Sarajevo and give a lecture on minority literature.

My retired Serb friend Ileana is selling her furniture to feed herself because of the economic embargo on Serbia which I once told her I support.

My Bosnian Serb friend Dragoslav edited and translated a wonderful anthology of pirated Canadian poetry.

My Macedonian friend Julija translated my 'Postcard Translations' into Macedonian but the wars broke out anyway.

My Serb friend the manager of the Smederevo winery hosted

the writers banquet because all winemakers are poets.

My nameless Kosovo friends are on their bar stools where I left them, very drunk, gesturing obscenely to Serb soldiers and/or the mountains.

My Serb friend Dusko phones from Belgrade to ask about my children and if I will come and lecture on multiculturalism.

My Serb friend Ileana last saw her parents and sister in Novi Sad in 1940 being led by Hungarian militia toward the river. She insists to me she is not 'political.'

I naively write back that politics is the opposite of shooting.

My Macedonian friend the bus driver stopped me in downtown Skopje so he and his wife could practice their English.

My Serb friend, a young actress, insisted she could be both sexy and Marxist.

My Slovene friend Mirko brought a bottle of plum brandy to me in Grainau.

My Dubrovnik friends got up at 6 AM to cook us bacon, eggs, sausage and tomatoes.

My Serb friend Mitrovic was on Belgrade television denying ethnic cleansing.

My Montenegron friend Katica is most likely still safe in Rijeka.

My Croat friend Angelika worked at the Zagreb TV station which my daughter saw burning on the Tuesday news.

My Serb friend Borjanka gave me dollars to buy her some English gin at the duty free store.

These could still be my friends in the ex-Yugoslavia.

Dead In Canada

i

There are a lot of dead people in Canada if you know where to look. I helped Greg dig into the riverbank below his house and we found slag from a foundary, veneer from a cabinet factory, and charred yellow bricks tossed over the edge by unhappy dead people. Regionalists have an advantage. Greg Curnoe made long lists of dead people, some of them painters, some of them hunters or clan mothers, and some of them brick-tossers who had owned his house. He disliked obscurity. He would talk about dead people as if they were alive. He would go to graveyards to look for them, or interview really old people. He thought if he wrote about them, or painted their words in pure colours, might they come back from being dead?

Greg never talked about death but he talked a lot about dead people. Dead people who once pitched horse-shoes on the lot next to his house. Dead steamship passengers who had died in his river. Dead tribesmen who some thousands of years ago had chipped away at arrowpoints and left small flakes of chert below his back lawn. Once he stopped to take a picture of an eighteenth-century house on the river near Chatham and the not-too-old owner invited us over and showed us bullet holes she had found in the south wall. Greg was real pleased because the holes had been made 180 years ago by a bunch of American dead guys.

iii

Entering Greg's studio the first thing you might have seen was a big full-length mirror. The new unit of poetry is not the foot or syllable I told him, it's the sentence. Greg used the mirror while painting like the rest of us use mirrors while driving a car. People used to think he used the mirror only to paint self-portraits but he also used it to paint words. The words, like his self-portraits, came from somewhere behind him but with his mirror he could keep putting them in front of us.

iv.

Look here he would say and then look somewhere else. In his studio there were all kinds of places to look. His studio was either all foreground or all background. A huge room with painting places and bicycle spaces and writing places and sleeping spaces and painting storage places but no sightlines and no perspective. The lawnmower usually sat beside the mirror. Or was it all kinds of sightlines and all kinds of perspectives. Look here he would say and then look behind him.

v.

In his studio there was a lot of dead people's stuff. In the neo-classical period, most artifacts were viewed as curios. Toy boats that had been made by dead people. Pictures taken by dead people. Signboards from the shops of dead people. What overjoyed Greg about the dead was that they could be so particular. In the nineteenth century artifacts became exhibits, to be organized in museums with good sightlines. Greg's old particulars lay all about, mixed up on his work tables with brushes and wrenches and rags and worn-out bike sprockets and hammers and exacto knives and little pots with dried-up watercolour. While this looks like a list, Greg's old stuff was not a list, it was things strewn about like a pile of old particular shoes. Often there was an imprecise dog in the pile of old shoes.

vi.

Did I mention all the watercolours of different sunsets?

vii.

We used to talk about whether all the talk of Canada was talk about old shoes. You can't be serious, he said, putting down his NCL edition of Anna Jameson. He'd been trying to fit a xerox of a Prudence Heward painting into his huge new watercolour. He'd been trying to fit Tecumseh into the history of his house. History can be a life narrative. He'd once painted Miss Supertest. A life-size action portrait of George Chuvalo. Canada is dead meat, I teased him, reminding him of the turkey vulture we had seen rising from Highway 2 just west of Pain Court. That was a Canadian turkey vulture he said.

The problem is that there are more things in the past to consider than in the future. Despite earthquakes fire and sword. There are databases of stuff about the past. Futurists to interpret it. Pastiches to continue it. Curators to present it. Greg had books in every room—books about the Russian Formalists, the French Impressionists, the German Expressionists, the American economists, the Italian Futurists. All of the paintings he owned were Canadian. In two small red and black books embossed *Cash* and *Records,* which he'd hand-subtitled 'About Painters,' he'd created five-star ratings of the past. Art criticism privileges individualist cultures. Given Claude Monet two stars. Joseph Beuys six stars. Hans Arp one star. Egon Schiele, 'drawings only,' three stars. How many medieval painters can you name? How many Sri Lankan? Given Beuys his fourth star on September 2nd 1988, his fifth on September 8, his sixth the next year on October 10th. But I am here, Greg reasonably replied, & then laughed because he was painting his ninteenth watercolour of 'it is me.'

The past needed sorting and resorting. Erich Heckel 4 stars. Books also on the War of 1812, the death of Wolfe, the 1837 rebellions, the death of Tecumseh. Claude Tousignant 4 stars. C'mon, he'd said, a few weeks after I'd come to London, I'll drive you around and show you the city. A strong sense of loss, little sense of time passing. Gustave Courbet 1 star. We drove back and forth across the river. Wisdom is a relative. His mom and dad's first house. Fred Varley 3 stars. The ponds nearby from the eighteenth-century river bed. His grandmother's house. Paul Gauguin 2 stars. The street where he grew up. His first school, Wortley Road Public. Natalia Goncharova 2 stars. Tecumseh School, his brother and sister's first school, and which he liked to pretend was his also. Wished was his also. The back of Jamelie Hassan's childhood home, beside the river. The great flood of 1883 that moved the main channel and destroyed 4 houses. Kurt Schwitters 3 or 4 stars. The bend in the river where the steamship *Victoria* capsized. Chris Dewdney's family home. J.M.W. Turner 2 stars.

X.

Highway 2 was Greg's favorite highway, and it was almost a dead highway. Once it had been the overland supply route from the fort at Detroit to Fort York and Kingston. Then other dead guys built it into the main east-west Ontario highway. Now the 401 expressway had nearly killed it. Greg loved Highway 2 because it was so dead you could cycle on it for miles without meeting much more traffic than a circling turkey vulture. Because it had markers for dead villages and plaques for dead heroes and parks for dead guys' battlefields. It went past reservations for tribes that dead nineteenth-century politicians expected by now to be dead. Near the Delaware reservation where his friends Daryl Stonefish and Diane Snake lived Greg was made dead. He was riding his bicycle with his bicycling friends on a nearly dead highway. Life came down the highway so fast and without looking and now to find Greg you go to a cemetery where he used to go to read the head-stones and find out what the dead could say about the living. Irony is what the dead leave to ease the pain of the living.

xi.

The older you get the more likely you are to write about the dead. Dead companions remain companions. When I visited I used to like to snoop in his expensive art books on Larionov and Kirschner. Greg wanted to know about the Indians who had mysteriously sold his city lot to the British Empire or who had defended it against Americans. Now the studio is quiet. His new computer, he'd discovered, would arrange long lists of words into alphabetical order. Or about white people who had farmed or made things where he now made lists of words on his city lot. E.L. Kirschner 3 or 4 stars. His new computer would make French accents. Now the expensive art books, which had once turned dead artists into royalties, dividends, and luminous patches of Canadian paint, are where I last left them. Now 'now' is simply now. Not then. Edgar Dégas 2 stars. He could look across the river from his upstairs window and see each south-facing window of the hospital where he was born. Paul Cézanne 3 stars. He could look in Pierre Théberge's not very expensive book and see a black-and-white photo of Greg Curnoe's painting of the hospital where people he knew were dying and being born. Greg was most particular. *View of Victoria Hospital, Second Series.* Around the year 1500 the population of the land within the present London city limits was 5,000. All now dead. He'd added numbers and labels to the hospital painting to announce what paint could not signify. Food cultivation allowed much larger settlements. Life and death exceed conventions. Vladamir Tatlin 7 stars. To know was to write and ride and paint etc. Now three pencils, seven brushes and a spoke wrench are stacked beside his easel. He could look down to the river and see the old Neutral corn fields. Greg Curnoe 6 rows of 12 stars.

The day he took me to the Tecumseh monument near Moraviantown was the day we saw the turkey vulture. Both were on Highway 2. Schools, some say, should be named after dead or retired role models. A family in a car from Michigan had pulled into the empty parking lot in front of us. They had been travelling east, like the Americans in 1813. This monument, a rusticly carved sign reads, was erected on the Thames battlefield in 1967 by Parks Canada. Greg asked what are they doing here, as if Sheila or I might know. That had also been the question in 1813, although after 30 years of moving and rebuilding their villages Tecumseh and his warriors may have thought they knew an answer. Maybe they are visiting *all* the historic places, said Sheila. Professional lawns, varnished picnic tables, and another sign 'Anyone defacing this site will be prosecuted.' General Proctor no stars. We followed the Americans to the monument but could hear only a bit of what they were saying. Carefully tended flower borders. Is somebody buried here? the boy asked his father. The old monument was better, it was Victorian, I don't know why they wrecked it Greg said. Greg always likes the old things Sheila said. After the battle the previous Americans had paraded Tecumseh's head on a fence pole. It was Sheila who had wanted him to get a home computer. I do not, Greg said.

For years Highway 2 went right across southern Ontario from Windsor to Cornwall. At Moraviantown, just up the road from the Tecumseh monument, the visitor can re-live its 1813 burning by Americans. Greg hoped the museum shop there would have a copy of Gray's *Wilderness Christians*. It did. The battlefield of Crysler's Farm, 300 km. to the east, is also on Highway 2. The foundations of the village have been carefully exposed and labelled. We wandered through, but without checking the precise positions of the opposing armies. Highway 2 followed historic trade and invasion routes across southern Ontario. Greg was excited that he'd got his book, and got it on Highway 2. Tecumseh's men and the British soldiers had been outnumbered 3 to 1. Picnic facilities are available at the Moraviantown site also. The Longwoods battlefield is also on Highway 2, but closer to London, and closer also to the hill where Greg died.

Because I kept visiting Greg I had to visit his dogs, who barked fiercely at all his visitors. It's okay they're real friendly, he'd propose, pushing them back from the door with his foot. Once I was walking across Greg's kitchen to get a beer and Lulu, his friendly Dalmatian, grabbed my right arm in her teeth. I had my leather jacket on, the one some have described as made from the skins of dead animals, and so I held up my arm with the dog hanging off by its overweight teeth and said Greg, look at this. Greg called, Sheila, hey look, Lulu is gumming Frank's arm. He seemed about to reach for his camera or paintbrush. Or for his rubber-stamps: LULU GUMS FRANK'S ARM. Lulu's jaws must have got tired, because she let go and wandered over to her water dish. When Sheila came in I had got my beer and I showed her the teeth marks on my dead animal jacket. Later I used to sit on Lulu's spot on the couch, and she would come and sit on top of me and fall asleep. Lulu gummed Frank's arm, Greg used to say whenever he had to introduce the two of us.

Greg's last big plan had been to visit the Egon Schiele collections in Vienna. He had a grant from the Canada Council, and his flight and hotel booked. Greg's most notorious painting had been his Dorval airport mural with its portrayals of Vietnam and Lyndon Johnson. Schiele of course was dead, and dead a lot younger than Greg could be. The mural is now dead, refused, de-commissioned, in storage at the National Gallery. Greg admired Schiele, Kirschner, and Heckel because they were all nasty outsiders. In twelve years Schiele had painted more self-portraits than Rembrandt had in fifty. Each self-portrait is a story like this one. In Vienna between 1906 and 1918 it could be difficult to avoid becoming dead. Greg had visited the Kirschner and Heckel collections in Cologne and Berlin in 1976 and two years later seen Schiele's 'Nude Against a Coloured Background' at the Stadt Galerie in Graz. Schiele's most notorious paintings were of himself masturbating. And most testing of his concentration. He died, 3 days after his wife, in the influenza epidemic of 1918. Greg admired Schiele, Pechstein, and Nolde because of their raw and pure and not-very-famous colours. The full-length mirror in Greg's studio was even larger than the celebrated one in Schiele's. Compare Greg's self-portrait no. 11 with Schiele's 'Self-Portrait Screaming.' Greg had wanted to go to Vienna to look in a dead man's mirror. Each self-portrait tells a new story. Notoriety comes from power, or fear of power. Schiele dying with his screams and semen. Johnson dying with his soldiers.

One night Greg asked me to stay for dinner because he was cooking. He had some new cemetery records of the Gumb family which had been one of his dead neighbours. After he died Sheila had to fill out a form that would tell an actuary how much he had cooked and mowed the lawn and fixed tap washers. The form was titled 'Loss of Handiman's Services—Compared to Known Others.' That night Greg had decided to serve fried chicken and boiled potatoes. In 1851 John Gumb had owned a bunch of land including the land under Greg's house and studio. Sheila impatiently ticked off Greg's handiman services and when the form reached the actuary it said that Greg had cleaned the Curnoe toilets three times a day. When Greg got the chicken and potatoes cooking he went to the fridge to look for a frozen vegetable. A man from the actuary's office phoned Sheila in great puzzlement. The census called John Gumb a widower and a brickmaker. All Greg could find in the fridge was frozen hashbrowns. We all tried to imagine Greg armed with a toilet brush and as obsessed with keeping three toilets clean as he was obsessed with doing a new painting or with tracking down details about dead neighbours, and it was easy. Much more particular than known others. Afterward we congratulated Greg, and told him this was our first meal ever of chicken with potatoes and potatoes.

After he died I dreamed I was back in his studio and that he was back too. He was joyous because he had started a collection of encyclopedias. Encyclopedias, I thought as I tried to remember the dream, are they really Greg? His collections were locally omnivarous and sometimes fortuitous but not encyclopedic. Metonymy sidesteps completeness. He was showing me three new sets he had just acquired. Sometimes he had showed me new books he'd bought about settler history or Georgia O'Keefe. Sometimes a new volume of the *Dictionary of Canadian Biography*. Then I noticed that each of his new sets of encyclopedia had a volume missing. That's how come I could get them cheap he'd explained. I thought in the dream, but didn't say, because Greg was so pleased with his finds, that he'd never find the missing volumes. He must have been reading my dreaming because right then he said isn't it better to have something that isn't everything than have nothing at all? After the dream I thought what you are probably thinking:

that death is a missing volume. Death leaves a room with unfilled volume. Then I went back to sleep and to dreaming. I dreamed I was jogging with Greg on the north side of Dufferin Ave. just east of my house, and we got separated a few steps before William Street, and so I jogged home to wait. When I stopped waiting I was right here and had found two dreams about Greg.

xviii. 'I was having breakfast. The sun was shining. 11 o'clock. November 14, Saturday.'

Greg became more famous by painting and writing and becoming dead than he had by painting and writing. Tom Thomson 6 stars. So much life after death: a blue historical plaque for his house, TV cameras outside the funeral, a *Globe and Mail* ready with obituary. The guy who absent-mindedly bashed the roof of his pick-up truck into Greg's bike-helmet was also shocked to have become so life-like, so imaginable. He had driven his truck smack-dab into an all-too-new Canadian painting. Gzowski phoned me from the big city. Front-cover articles in *Canadian Art* and *C-Magazine*. A Curnoe tree in Harris Park. Greg had been cycling through a strange landscape, a barn seemingly floating on a flooded field. At the funeral a turn-away crowd. His Toronto show a week later later his first sell-out. Fame after fortune. On another occasion, he might have stopped, slipped off his backpack, and sketched a particular barn watercolour. Instead retrospectives at the London Regional and National

Galleries. A Curnoe bicycle tunnel to Greenway Park. Some day at the foot of a slight rise on Highway 2 there will be a monument saying 'Here died Greg Curnoe.' A parking lot, a few flowers and picnic tables. A professional lawn. Is somebody buried here an American kid will ask. Canadians will slow their canoes and bicycles. If I am not dead I will try again to remember.

Italian Multiculturalism

At the fifteenth biennial conference of the Italian Association for Canadian Studies, hosted by the University of Venice, everyone hates multiculturalism.

Piazza San Marco is filled with pigeons and tourists from twenty-one nations all eager to see the classical Greek horses, or their modern replicas, whichever, in the cathedral.

On the Riva degli Schiavoni young Ethiopians stroll in the May sunshine hawking Asian-made Rolexes and Louis Vuiton bags just like in Paris, or Athens, or Seville.

But the conference is not being held in Venice, it is being held in the flat farmland northwest of Venice, in Monastere de Treviso, and the converted monastery many of the Canadians had expected is a large motel with meeting rooms and a weedy rose garden.

'Le multiculturalism menaçant,' nous dit Monique Proulx.

Well you know them Kweebeckers.

*

Yesterday I nearly lost myself my passport in the Piazzale Roma.

I had been enjoying the sunshine on the Grand Canal, and walking the back streets between Rialto and San Marco.

I had put my passport and my wallet and my map all into the one inside pocket of my leather jacket.

Every time I pulled out my wallet, like to buy tickets for the vaporetto, the passport and map came out with it.

Back near San Marco I checked for my wallet as I calmly do

every ten seconds whenever I'm outside of multicultural Canada. It and my map were there but my passport was gone.

I must have accidentally pulled the passport from my pocket while buying postcards at the south end of the piazza.

I began looking for a Canadian consulate.

My passport, my wife pointed out, was lodged between the waistband of my leather jacket and my well-filled stomach.

*

A huge multicoloured pile of bags, suitcases, and garment cases in the hotel lobby.

At the conference finance table, prominently located outside the bar, the newly arrived argue in vain to be allowed to pay their hotel and meal costs with credit cards or deutschmarks or dollars canadiens. Me too.

We must each be a 'nation of one' announces Timothy Findley.

Janice Kulyk Keefer arrives with news of yesterday's Canadian studies conference in Jerusalem.

Outside in the flat fields and vineyards it is starting to rain. In the bar a bunch of the guys are whooping it up watching CNN.

I wish I were back in Venice losing my passport.

The Canadian and Québec governments don't give enough money to artists, who are indispensible citizens, says Marie-Claire Blais.

I find my Knirps umbrella and walk a half mile down the

78

road to the Farmer's Savings Bank (my translation) and buy half a million lira on my Bank of Montreal gold Mastercard.

I get the Union Jack and Made in Malaya labels on my Reeboks soaked.

Minority lobby groups and state fascism are equally the enemies of good writing, says Timothy Findley. Each writer is one voice, he says. 'Susan Swan, Alberto Manguel, Nourbese Philip, Joy Kogawa,' he says, 'voices.'

Susan Swan and Alberto Manguel applaud. Back in Ontario Nourbese Philip and Joy Kogawa are about to eat their North American breakfasts.

The first evening dinner is served an hour later than scheduled because the opening speeches have been longer. That is, there have been many voices.

'Singing is in my Irish blood,' says Timothy Findley.

Rural buses to downtown Treviso pass every forty minutes.

A glass of Albano helps dissolve overcooked risotto.

'My voice will still be alive even when I'm a dead white male,' says Timothy Findley. The Italian students look puzzled.

The next morning the young old hopeful confident Italian female male Québécois German nervous Canadian academics begin giving their papers. All the papers are long.

'L'écrivain est une solitaire,' nous dit Marie-Claire Blais, 'qui crée une littérature universale.'

Each male Italian professor of Canadian studies wants to present a paper and also to have each of his students present a paper.

Literature explores everything life can offer, says Alfredo

Rizzardi.

Consequently there is no time for discussion after any of the papers.

Each new Canadian constituency writes from a different aesthetic and perspective, says Branko Gorjup.

Lunch is late, the food cold.

Multiculturalism undermines nationalism, complains Rick Salutin.

Writers can be paralyzed, Catriona Edwards says, when they learn that the self is a social construction. The papers continue.

The conference banquet is held in a Renaissance palace about 40 km from Monastere. The bus gets lost on the way. We arrive at dusk and enter along a winding dimly lit path through a large garden. 'A brooding Renaissance palace' at least one Canadian writes in his journal. At the banquet there is polenta, risotto, risi e bisi, spaghetti, fegato alla veneziana, costolletta, baccala, fagioli, costata and some of it is warm and one of the banquet rooms is cold and the other warm and both have gardens and angels and cherubs painted on the walls and ceiling.

This event has not been very Canadian, Rick Salutin tells his table, there have been no arguments, no denunciations of Americans.

Sure beats rubber chicken.

Some Italian scholars see conferences not as a place to debate or confer, says Branko, but to compete for status in the number of their students who give papers.

Lise Gauvin says that Québec writers must re-territorialize their language. Applause.

Catriona Edwards says that literary theory holds back younger writers by making them feel stupid. Applause.

Timothy Findley says that minority-group protests are, like Naziism, an enemy of good writing. Applause.

On the final morning a crowd of participants gather around the finance table where the organizers are giving away spectacular colour posters of a Colville painting.

Fortunately, no racial-minority Canadian writers have been invited.

The last session is a literary reading back in Venice at the university's own renaissance palace, the Ca'Foscari. My wife takes a vaporetto to the Lido.

Susan Swan tells us that in Canada 'politically correct' means that the characters in a work of fiction are all morally perfect.

Connie Rooke reports that in Canada literary beauty is endangered.

Timothy Findley says 'Political correctness stinks.'

In the evening, my wife and I have dinner at a quiet ristorante on a canal bank near the Papadopoli Gardens.

From across the Adriatic we can almost hear various Serbs, Croats, and Bosnians trying not to be morally perfect, or to endanger beauty.

The next morning we catch a train for Strasbourg, where another conference begins the day after.

The boatmen charge us $100 to take our luggage across the Grand Canal to the rail station.

I fumble in the black leather fanny-pack my wife bought for me and my passport in the market below Rialto.

84

The Eurotrain flies with equal smoothness across Hannibal's, Caesar's, or Kesselring's battlefields.

In Kolmar we stop to see the Grunewald altarpiece, in whose panels thousands are voluptuously dying.

Lust, gluttony, covetousness, pride.

The conference subtitle was 'Quale Canada Domani?'

Some call the altarpiece a unique individual achievement, and some a pinnacle of medieval art.

Translating History

The Villa Kérylos

'Don't be too sanguine, Mrs. Moodie.'

1. Proauleion/sunporch/verandah/stoop

Every notebook and masterwork needs a verandah. The house which Dr. Reinach began in 1902 on the Mediterranean just east of Nice was to be the house from which all Western dwellings descend, the model for our family aspirations. Only the finest materials could be chosen—marble, fruitwood, porphyry, teak, ivory, opaline, plaster of marble dust. By the 1960s Kérylos was, like Versailles before it, empty and mildewed, virtually a dead house which only a moribund state could wish to repair. An astonishing waterfront setting. Kérylos: halcyon, sea-swallow. A monument to one man's devotion or obsession. Its blind back wall to the street, its porch facing the rocks and waves, Kérylos distills our knowledge of the domestic architecture of the ancient world, captures forever its graces and traditions. An archaeologically precise model. Against a background of Princess Grace hillsides. Although rightly choosing the Age of Pericles, Dr. Reinach wisely dismissed the windowless homes of Athens for the spacious villas of the Aegean seafarers, whose wide windows surveyed the sea in all directions for returning ships. Completed in 1908, Dr. Reinach's building became in 1967 an 'ancient monument of France' because the government needed to explain its financing of a total restoration.

2. Thyroreion/vestibule/mudroom

This is the beginning, the entrance, the start of it all, happy new year, the gateway, inevitably gendered. In Canadian houses this room is often a glassed-in porch, with cat-food dishes, gardening shoes. 'The effect was strangely novel and imposing.' At

Kérylos, here is where the bureaucrats, and now the tourists, under garlands of bougainvillea, enter. Many ambiguous symbols of friendship. A large bronze serpent, symbol of health. Ubiquitous men in uniform, a change of flags, black-framed photos of a head of state. Overhead a fresco of Mars, triumphant. As soon as Dr. Reinach arrived at his villa he donned ancient Greek robes, and required his all-male houseguests to follow his example. A haphazard pile of riding boots, awaiting an invisible servant. In the sunporch he had wisely placed a life-size statue of Sophocles, who stood amazed at such drama, such tragic fiction.

3. Peristyle/courtyard/patio/deck

In this room the ideal house begins. Twelve columns arranged in a square to surround a marble fountain and a rose laurel. The billboard fantasies of Greek tourism, private gardens, sunlit

Ionic columns, recreated by international hotels. Or the courtyards of the shopping mall, asking you to forget the street and the noisy outdoor sun. Most classical villas had two courtyards, the second perhaps for the women. Dr. Reinach's mosaic floor suggests an eternal and low-upkeep garden. Here we must think we can forget the sports page, the Deutschmark, underwater archaeology in Hudson's Bay, families that will never get to move to the suburbs. Leafy vines in the paintwork lead the eye nowhere. Every stone surface reproaches the shoppers in the next street poking at melons. The windows indeed look only seaward. On the hills above Nice the equivalent is the ten-foot masonry wall around the garden, or the house built in three wings against the lot line. From the very beginning was the private house at war with public space. Now no one sits in a tank-top on the proauleion sipping beer and shouting proverbially at the neighbour. There is time and a doorway in this courtyard for everything—six hours alone with Homer, six in your very own Hippocrates gym and spa. A storybook sun, god of the arts and music, spells out Dr. Reinach's hours of labour and rest.

4. Amphithyros/front hall/foyer/atrium

What do we say of the everyday accumulations on our bodies of places and things? Here is the vestibule all over again. If you re-invent the world in marble, then you must start your house all over again within it. Even the dog licks itself. A house you are forever entering. Each space has its codes and decorums. You pass yet another front door and the daily odors of the house rise from its rugs and curtains, its sofas and lampshades, even from the woodgrains of the doors and windows. And everyone but you is unclean. Or exotic. Or this is a theatre among theatres, the doors open only upon a stage, there are things 'written'. The teenage girl in the ruins of Shattila, New Years 1992, asked 'What is written for us?—we are afraid because we do not know what is written for us.' The host is seldom afraid. 'Over the white marble basin he has placed the gargoyle of a lion's head, to remind the guest to purify himself.' Sic. On the opposite wall stands a copy of a copy of the Athena once carved by someone to whom memory has given the name of Phidias. This is the same memory who on another day named Athena and on another—do you remember?—invented the syllables for memory. This is a busy house, and we may not know whether to attend to the lion or Athena, or whether Athena wants us to attend to the lion.

5. Library/bookroom/den/study

The library is not a place to curl up with a good book. There are no books visible in Dr. Reinach's balconied library. Large enough for a game of pick-up basketball. Most prominent is the white marble floor, the stars and crosses of its gold and black inlays. Beyond this point absolutely no food or drink are permitted. Most prominent are the fruitwood and leather reproductions of Greek chairs and three-legged tables. Your book will be overdue in 10 days. Visitors would unconsciously run their fingers along the wood-grains or nestle their shoulders further into the leather. Most prominent are the Roman amphora and the Corinthian and Etruscan vases that Dr. Reinach acquired from restricted archaeological sites. Books left on tables overnight will be collected and returned to their shelves. These windows look east over the Bay of Beaulieu toward Eze and Monte Carlo, making it easier to work in the morning and protecting papyri from the setting sun. Silence. Outside are solitary flowers with a gaping two-lipped corolla. Dr. Reinach's writing desks are all more than four feet high because he had learned that the ancient Greeks wrote standing up. On the admirably collonaded balcony curtained cupboards conceal the scrolls that remember the voice of the graceful Nanno.

6. The triklinos/dining room

The formal dining room is an option in Canadian architecture. Dr. Reinach followed the Greek practice of having the men,

95

and the women with their children, dine separately. Imagine instead Hollywood scenes of a Roman banquet, with the guests lounging on sofas and cushions beside low tables. Without women, without dogs. Twenty years ago this grey and white mosaic floor would have been a triumph of op art. After the men had purified themselves, and dressed in Greek garb/duds/ gear, they reclined on the leather couches while servants piled the three-legged tables with grapes and lamb. The chandeliers of tiny oil lamps recreate those of the Hagia Sophia, but have been quietly electrified. Many Canadian families close off their dining rooms except for Easter and Christmas. A few enjoy talking loudly of their nanny and separate adults' and children's tables. Class ambitions in all sizes. Some guests might prefer the children's table. I asked our guide where Dr. Reinach ate when he had no male guest but she replied that such a question was not part of the tour. After dinner he carried his glass of port to the Andron.

7. The andron/study/(with)drawing room/den

This is the room that gives the world androcentrism, androgeny, polyandry, androids. It's a man's world, my mother used to tell me. The walls are panelled with rose-coloured marble from Serravezza, otherwise called peach-blossom. Chauvinism was always easier for the rich. The best my dad could do was his lodge hall. The mosaic floor of this room is a geometric maze at the centre of which Theseus joyfully wrestles the minotaur. Ariadne is not allowed here. It's a man's world, she'd say, not so much as a protest than as a sign of unhappy wisdom. Etruscan pots overflow with dried flowers. Most ordinary Greeks lived in cubicle blocks. The largest chair is a Greco-Egyptian throne reserved for Dr. Reinach. I look in vain for spittoons and ashtrays. The minotaur joyfully wrestles Theseus. The room that was most my dad's was his basement workshop, but this was also the laundry room. He could smoke in any room he wanted. I asked the guide if Dr. Reinach smoked or allowed smoking, since tobacco was unknown in classical Greece. The guide was a cute female student from the university who did not want to appear intimidated by bearded questioners. It's a man's world, my mother sighed, and I admit I was glad to hear it.

8. Oikos/living room/back parlour

My own house, built by a petroleum merchant in 1873, has a front and back parlour. The Oikos of Dr. Reinach is dedicated, the guide says, to an extremely cheerful Dionysus. Small serving tables of citrus wood inlaid with ivory. Although this room is less than half the size of the andron. We use our back parlour as a TV and dog grooming room, and keep the front parlour shut except for house parties. Otherwise our cat pees in it. The Oikos mosaic depicts grapes being harvested by sileni, fauns, and satyrs, although even in Dr. Reinach's time actual grapes were harvested by underpaid labourers. The drama of a good house denies work. My house has servants rooms at the back, out of sight, above the kitchen. The Oikos walls reproduce the masks of tragedy, comedy, and tragicomedy that survived in the theatre at Pergamun. I had childhood friends whose parents never allowed them in the living room. The genius of Dr. Reinach was that he recognized a house's theatrical function, its message to the Joneses. Modern transportation enables workers to be kept on the other side of a city. The beauty of a marble surface is that it betrays not a chisel blade, a hammer stroke. For the Victorians the front parlour could present your life, or death, as you wished it. For Dr. Reinach, the back parlour could also conceal, within a citrus cupboard, a grand piano, not invented until 1720.

9. Gynaeceum/rec room/rumpus room/family room

This is the room that doesn't appear on any official house maps. The kids hang out here while upstairs the adults swap drinks with Dionysus. In Dr. Reinach's notion of a Greek house, remember, the adults are men. This is where the piano should have been, except that one of the doctor's frequent male visitors was Gabriel Fauré. I didn't see this room when I toured Kérylos, so I began having paranoid delusions that something was being hidden. In St. Catharines, the Homolka's rec room was where Paul and Karla wrecked her little sister. Dr. Reinach and his wife had four children. What happens when the men march into the romper room? Paul had sneaked in, pretending to be just one of the kids. The rec room is an all-purpose room, sometimes filled with toys, sometimes with empty glasses, bottles, and syringes. The other possibility is that Kérylos was not a house at all but a summer cottage where Dr. Reinach, his family back in Paris, could pretend to live like an ancient of Delos.

10. Bedrooms

Upstairs, the bedrooms, like the other major rooms, appear adorned for house beautiful. Most Greek and Roman houses I have seen mixed the bedrooms with the main floor rooms. All agents of this splendour too have vanished—the architect, the mason, the painter, and the chambermaid. The 'bird' bedroom glows with peacocks and swans painted for Hera. Dr. Reinach's 'loves' bedroom features a mosaic of Dionyus on his trireme, where he has just transformed various pirates into dolphins. Mirrors have disappeared, behind panels in the woodwork. Between the Hera suite and the loves suite, the 'triptolemos' slyly celebrates the world's first sharing of seedgrains. I found three bathrooms with solid marble basins but couldn't find a guest room. On the floor above, the servants' rooms have been converted into offices for the museum-staff. This separation of sleeping and daytime activity rooms may be a much later invention. Dr. Reinach's romantic imagination was refined but unoriginal. Two fluted Doric pillars framed his bed, like the pillars that frame the doorways of Edwardian banks. A lot of money invested in this bed, the original of which is in storage at the occasionally open Archaeological Museum of Naples.

11. The balaneion/bathroom/spa/hottub

Can one think of the bath as a principal social room? Splish splash. At the Comfort Inn in Rochester my wife rented us the 'Jacuzzi Room.' The house my family bought when I was one didn't have a bathroom. The jacuzzi of the Jacuzzi Room turned out to be hidden behind the bathroom's plywood door. Dr. Reinach's largest bathing room was called the Naiades. Its octagonal tub, a pool large enough for a dozen naiads or dryads, was recessed into more white marble. Except for hottubs and gay bathhouses, Canadians have forgotten the pleasures of communal bathing. The museum staff too display a certain ambivalence, making the visitor descend to the tub from the bedrooms, not from the rooms of public reception.

The tub's Carrera marble walls are streaked with gold. In the gold mosaic of its floor four golden fish pursue four golden weeds etc. Ordinary gold soap dishes, or maybe ashtrays, have been fixed to the tub's walls. Ionic columns of white and grey stone to frame the frolicking bathers. Even at the beach most of us swim alone. In his spare time my dad plumbed a small room with galvanized steel and cast iron. Ironic columns, my mother called them. Dr. Reinach and I may have seen a bath much like this at Pompei. This week the Ontario government reduced welfare allowances by 22%. Bathing in classical times was not necessarily done for cleanliness. Bathing is different from swimming. Did he have parties here, I asked the guide.

12. Kitchen.

When the French state took the house over its managers turned the basement kitchen into an exhibition room, and the root cellar into a lecture hall. The kitchen was the only room where Dr. Reinach had allowed technologies unknown to the ancients. Kitchens, he believed, are spaces without meaning. The Greeks had kept their kitchens in an obscure corner of the main floor because no one was supposed see them. Even today we locate our kitchens in the backs of our houses. Perhaps Madame Reinach drew a line at the kitchen, our guide suggested. Most of the kitchen staff in a classical Greek house would have been slaves. Because it is a famous house, Kérylos is now a house without a kitchen. The kitchen is also the room that stages the most obvious and intense scenes of work. The myth of Eden is the myth of comfort without labour. At Versailles, the king and courtiers endured cold food to keep the kitchen sounds ten minutes from their palace walls.

13. Exit

This is the end, na na na na, goodbye. Except at Kérylos there is no end, only a way back through the andron, the triklinos, the fake vestibule, the central square, the entrance hall, the sunporch, and out to the Riviera day. My favorite houses know the value of a good exit. A slam of the carport door. A quick shinny off the back porch roof. This is the end. The rotting roof falls through, the coffered ceilings collapse, the marbled plaster peels in November's rain. Except now there is to be no end. The state's perpetual care encodes the house in a Grecian urn, with the Leacock house, Chambord, Cluny, Jenny Butchart's gardens. This is the end. Two old people huddled in a pristine and gilded tub. Bleached walls around the nearby houses. Walls and locks around the neighbourhoods of houses. The vestibule mosaics of Pompei shout to the houseguest 'Cave Canis' in an assortment of breeds. Car alarms warble. Nurses scurry.

14. The Basse Corniche

Except it is not the end. The visitor leaves, can run under the palm trees, toss stones into the Baie des Fourmis. The perfect house is behind, already a museum, standing only because of subsidy. The windows should have been of parchment, but Dr. Reinach was afraid of the wind, and in love with a silent vista. That ten percent of Canadians earn eighty percent of their nation's wealth tells that ten percent of Canadians are subsidized by ninety. Kérylos descends less from Delos than from Strawberry Hill. Sprawling suburbs underwrite the suburban house. In Canada the contemporaries of Kérylos are Hatley Park, The John Labatt House, Casa Loma, all either demolished or state property. Polluted air helps fuel the commuters' autos. Beware of privilege, rip-off, decorative art. The cubicle block is the model from which most housing rises. In Bavaria, Dr. Reinach's contemporary is Mad King Ludwig. Most photos of Kérylos are taken from Cap Ferrat, site of a Rothschild museum, a zoo, heavily guarded villas, and a lycée canadienne.

Translating from the Greek

1. *There once was once a snake in the Erichtheon*

All through Greece the three of us had been exchanging. Talents into dollars. Greek letters into 'autoroute.' Autoroute into extra wide 2-lane highway. Ruins into old cities the size of villages. Now I am extra glad to be alive. I can find the German words for 'fusebox' and 'alternator' but not the Greek words. In the smoky grey sky far beyond the Erichtheon the thunder had rumbled. I'd easily translated it into sound effects. I is also the map translator—while his wife drives. On the streets toward the streets toward the road out of Athens the rain had poured, the gutters swelled. *Blitzen,* I now try to say, in the present language of profit and travel. The wipers had raced to change raincrash to streetscape. Me to change floodwater to roadway. I'll just follow the other cars she'd said. It is no easy task to embrace the economies of Hellas.

2. *In the Morning*

We had arrived on the overnight ferry from Crete, parked high in a three-story gas station, taken a taxi to the Acropolis. For a traveller, even gas-pumps can be theatrical. The driver had once been a dairy farmer, of black and white cows from Canada. He would rather be farming. Along the highway from Piraeus there had been nothing pastoral, small shops, factories, and billboards for movies with suntanned actresses. Canada is very good for black and white cows, he said. He was quitting taxi-driving forever this weekend. Nineteenth-century engravings show cows and sheep of various colours grazing beside the Parthenon. Can you keep your taxi to use as a car, I asked him. Yes, but I have to change engine, he said. Diesels permitted now only for taxis. He pointed to the sky, where splendid stagey clouds were swirling. Too much black, too much smoke he said.

3. *A Pleasant Town*

Modern Delphi in springtime is a pleasant town. I had been glad to be alive before, but not at the same level of consciousness. Hotels on the lower street overlook three thousand years of olive groves in the Pleistos valley, and beyond the Gulf of Corinth. We were often the only ones in the restaurant and so could always get a window table. *Apollo had brought the Muses down from their home on Mount Helicon to Delphi, had tamed their wild frenzy.* After two millenia visitors calmed and slowed by the mountain vistas are still the main industry. And indeed there are no further storms, we are even surprised at how well the car runs. Conversely we had visited Olympia without becoming athletes. Linda had stood centre-stage at Epidaurus and spoken softly to our daughter and me as we sat centre-high among the seats, and that had been not at all the same as being cured of illness. Not even carried back in time. At Knossos we had entered and left the labyrinth—no bull. Now our questions are still ones of translation.

4. *Under a Cypress*

An old man in a mountain village on the backroad to Olympia who had tried to flag us down. But no one tried to direct us out of Athens. Travellers by definition are more often going than resting. Once I had thought I would live a long time, but as one lives the tenses alter. There were barricades across Athens' flooded boulevards. At the village garage I try to draw a picture of a thunderbolt. *Blitzen,* I remember. Fire can be variously interpreted as passion, anger, destruction, energy, or wisdom. We had thought the old man was selling rugs and hadn't wanted any. It's at Delphi not Olympia you can purchase information. *It seems that certain Northern Hellenes invaded central Greece and the Pellopenese, where they were opposed by the pre-Hellenic worshippers of the Earth-Goddess, but captured her chief oracular shrines.* Three hours to find the highway again northwest from Athens. Fire is a commodity many of us want, although if the old man had waved a flaming branch we would also not have stopped. It was almost as hard to get to Olympia as it is now to Delphi, although as far as we knew, we were in no danger. On the way we had seen more land turtles, three, than we'd seen cars. No black and white cows. The earth was so hot where the athletes had posed that Linda and Sara sat under a cypress and waited for me to finish looking. Ruins, trees and fantasy. The victors were given such riches they were fixed for life. We had stopped for the turtles and one of us, like a god worried about wealth or death, had lifted each to the roadside it had been facing.

5. *The Undershells of Turtles*

The undershells of the turtles were cool and smooth. Fire translates solids into gas, and liquids into vapors. Clambering up and down temples, Sara was getting a useful leg-up on Grade 12 history. Intervention translates direction into destination. At Mycenae our climb through the Lions gate had been unambiguous. *Apollo disguised himself as a tortoise, with which Dryope and her companions played, and when Dryope placed him on her bosom he turned into a hissing serpent, scared away the companions, and enjoyed her.* I knew I was getting old when I stood at Olympia's starting line and had no desire to sprint down the stadion. Linda and Sara sat waiting for me on one of the toppled pillars of Zeus's temple. Too much culture. The heat finally sent us scrambling back to the very profitable orange juice stand just outside the ticket booth.

6. *Driving to Parnassus*

On the narrow highway the rain intensifies, mixes with lightning forks, thunders on trees, mountain fields, our now resounding Toyota. Metaphors swirl the blurred windows eager for translation. Under the hood thunderbolts themselves have been translated into friendly electrolites. Each culture translates natural events into stories that fit the meanings and narratives of its everyday activities. Apollo, or the patriarchal culture of Apollo, translated Gaia's shrine into his own. When a thunderbolt strikes, the voltage regulator may attempt, unsuccessfully, to convert it to 12 volts. 'BOOM,' I write, in lame approximation. Apollo slew the fearsome female serpent of Gaia, but his followers soon translated it as male. And other stupid things, given the electrifying context, I'll be glad I don't say. Something about blue light. Sara is in the back seat and thinks we all are dead. I'm not sure about anything. Worshippers have tried to convert the thunderbolt into power by giving bribes, often called offerings, to the priests. Roman generals converted most of the Delphic offerings into booty. Linda shifts quickly from

5th to 3rd. Storms at sea converted some of the booty into lost treasure. Archaeologists can sometimes convert lost offerings into cultural information, and sometimes into tourists. Right now, Sara wants no changes at all. A philosopher might convert an offering into a trace, or philosophy into linguistics or anthropology into translation. The alternator light converts battery power to glow its own approching doom. We and our two and one-half remaining cylinders continue, not fearlessly, but because damn, it's wet out there. After thousands of years, thunderbolts offer the same paranoid inspirations ahead as behind. How freaky, how banal, Linda said.

7. *The Vale of Tempe* (interlude)

Such regional highways are lightly travelled. Far to the north the trees reach toward you from both mountainsides. Them women stick together. Today the visitor can drive effortlessly through sites of epic struggle or profound romance. The expected associations of clefts between hills. A government picnic site by the water-nymph's stream. Apollo was a sun god and his return to the vale was part of the annual cycle of light and shadow. Only with difficulty can one separate the grotto-like aspects of such sites (the Delphic spring, the Tempe vale) from the female actants believed to dwell there. Apollo took the vale. We couldn't see a bit of Olympus, or of any of the mountains, because of low clouds, disappointing rain. Apollo could barely distinguish Daphne from the mist. A table dancer, strutting her stuff on a rock. Apollo was the sign of newly tumescent power, herdsmen and farmers, who would soon return as bossmen of Delphi. I put my head out the window, we were deep in the mountains, there were indeed moist limbs, vaginal leaves. As far as the other male gods were concerned Apollo's games were misdemeanors, an epistemic shift, minor infractions. The story could have been very short. But them trees stick together. As soon as things get awkward, they yell for the great mother. Much ground foliage on both sides of the road. The residual attraction of matriarchy. For Apollo, his exile to Tempe and his disappointments there were but temporary setbacks.

8. *Some Roadside Services*

We, of course, were not exiled to Tempe. The Toyota would stumble a few miles onward. The village mechanic would repair the burned alternator. Multinational economics would have trucked to his shelf a replacement regulator. The Pythia would burn laurel leaves on the sacred hearth. The grammarian makes a point that frames my own. Suspecting now that messages may come in mysterious ways, the visitor makes sure that he has touched the Kastalian Spring. My wife finds the Greek word. The storm continues. People from the village come driving by anyway to stare at a foreign vehicle. Two hours later, between the village and Delphi we would pass bodies laid out beside a fatal collision. The clouds would swirl in their polluted postmodern patterns. The mechanics laugh and point at us each time thunder rocks the building. The event itself was both minor and cataclysmic. Disaster dribbles away in repair bills, anticlimax, and dependent clauses.

9. *The Seventh Day*

There is little to say about it now. Climbing the once sacred way, we have already passed the seventh day. *Apollo's oracles, which he did not deliver on his own initiative but as the mouthpiece of Zeus, were infallible*. Linda explains that the Lesbian wall was built by people from Lesbos, that is Lesbians of assorted sexualities. Even more likely, it was built by slaves. Sixteen gilded treasuries once held the official offerings. God of song and music, leader of the prosperous muses. I'm still nervous, there are rocks to trip over, half-broken columns to fall. Delphi, navel of the thundering world, was the wealthiest shrine of agricultural Greece. The clefts of the mountains soar around us. The Lesbian wall was built to protect Apollo's temple from earthquakes, boulders from which now litter the slope. We all look for change but may not be too happy about it when it happens. The numerous column bases are the remains, I read, of elaborate bronze and gold oblations. Perhaps I should have told Sara, who is a violinist, about the dying Marsyas's flute and Apollo's lyre. Each of the three of us must have our own relationship to lightning. Having lost the war for spring and thunder, the water-nymph and her priestesses fled to Crete where she became the moon goddess Pasiphae. It's a quiet day, and despite the occasional cloud, and our memories, only whispers of thunder. None of us were sure who, or how many, had been spoken to. I walk right past the omphalos, which was not only the navel stone but also the tomb of the Python, but Linda calls me back. Where the sacrificed beasts had shivered in their useful terror. Even the position of the ritual flame, extinguished now some sixteen centuries, cannot be reconstructed with certainty. I pause anyway. In the distance the faint horns of an election rally.

10. *Flames and Flashes*

Sudden cascades of electrons grip the mystery of a good story. Here at this ground zero a quiet breeze and the smell of pines. A blast that had surrounded us, a blue flame that swirled on the engine hood. A good story for Apollo can be now a lousy one for tourism. A blue flame that was never an answer and at best an indifferent demonstration. Once upon a moment a water-nymph had fled as three thousand years of lucrative theology flashed as if apocalyptically from a hidden sky. At 110 kph the flame's speed and position impossible to reconstruct with certainty. The mechanics had watched and laughed. The Python was undoubtedly and quickly killed. In the gulf far below a freighter moves toward Itea. Fiery engines rumble. The ruined treasuries of the new god glisten. Segues and sequiturs. We had been drawn to the theatre and discovered it a stage for an old economy. An Hitachi regulator had been on the shelf. It's an everyday choice whether to climb the much broken path to the stadion.

A Small History of Québec

10823 BC: first child born at Memphemagog.

10463 BC: first production of fluted spear points at Abitibi. Groundwork laid for future trade.

10329 BC: ivory toys produced at Mascogouche.

9760 BC: large-scale production of notched spearheads at Massiwippi.

9502 BC: first export of stone knives to Chappaquidick and Manhattan.

8987 BC: woodworking enterprises launched near Metabe-touan.

8024 BC: polished stone trade begins with Ottawa Valley.

7822 BC: first successful netting of fish in the Chicoutimi River. Groundwork laid for larger settlements.

7276 BC: grooved axe design perfected at Stadacona. Production under licence in Mississauga.

6546 BC: establishment of a small cemetery at Temiskaming.

5830 BC: copper tools imported from the Nipissing.

5344 BC: fish gaffs mass-produced at Maskinonge.

4820 BC: tubular tobacco pipes become new fashion.

4730 BC: fish weirs constructed on rapids west of Hochelaga.

4243 BC: hand-drills acquired in trading with Mahicans.

3927 BC: bow and arrow technology acquired from Canandaigua. Groundwork laid for agriculture.

3570 BC: large cemetery established at Arthabaska. Burials of dogs permitted.

3442 BC: traders from Susquehanna arrive with soapstone tableware.

3345 BC: polished stone jewelry and seashell trade begins at Rimouski.

2432 BC: ceramics production begins at Missiquoi for pipes and coil vessels.

1732 BC: copper beads become the rage at Raskatong.

1055 B.C: squash farming begins at Megantic.

420 BC: silver acquired from Temagami.

330 BC: thin wall ceramics produced at Shawinigan.

275 BC: shell-stamped ceramics developed at Manicougan. Matching sets become collectible in North Tonawanda.

322 AD: first maize seed imported from Saranac Lake.

732: house size increases as band populations grow.

1133: first Iroquois bands arrive in Hochelaga Valley.

1411: building of fortified village at Hochelaga.

1534: French travellers visit Micmac bands near Anticosti and Iroquois at Stadacona.

1542: unfriendly French travellers visit Hochelaga.

1567: Hochelagans and Stadaconans move to better land in Ontario.

1593 Montagnais and Askapi move to Stadacona, renaming it

'Quebec,' an Algonquin word which translates into French as 'a narrowing of the river.'

1603: French travellers set up tourism centre at 'Quebec.' Groundwork laid for Expo 67.

1609: Algonquins hire French mercenaries to assist in raid on Mohawks.

1615: Hurons hire French mercenaries to help in raid on Oneida.

1628: English visitors evict French travellers from 'Quebec' lodgings.

1632: French travellers return.

1634: Hurons and Algonquins acquire French guestworkers to help with food supply.

1642: Mohawks retain de Maisonneuve to rebuild Hochelaga, and Jeanne Mance to open hospital.

1643: Seneca and Mohawks import large stock of muskets from Amsterdam.

1653: Onondaga, Mohawks, and Seneca defeat and disperse Hurons and withdraw to south.

1663: Mohawk clan mothers engage Jean Talon to administer Hochelaga in their tribe's absence.

1668: Montagnais arrange for several hundred 'King's Daughters' (homeless young women refugees and prostitutes), to be sent from Paris to reduce sexual harrassment of Montagnais women by guestworkers and mercenaries.

1672: Illinois hire Marquette and Joliet to help open trade route to Hochelaga River.

1713: Iroquois and Algonquin negotiators at Utrecht peace talks secretly direct Louis XV to end French emigration to Quebec and Hochelaga.

1735: Cheyenne and Blackfoot engage La Vérendrye to help open trade route to Hochelaga River.

1755: Micmac expel local French guestworkers to Louisiana. Groundwork laid for Cajun cooking and myth of Evangeline.

1759-60: Iroquois stage successful British invasion to begin tribal return to Hochelaga Valley.

1761: Algonquin and Iroquois begin long-term campaign of intermarriage with French guestworkers. Call campaign 'revenge of the cradle.'

1763: Algonquin and Iroquois under Pontiac attempt hostile takeover of fur industry, but are defeated.

1774: disappointed on battlefield, Iroquois draw up 'Quebec Act' to expand range of aboriginal territory.

1783: while pretending to assist Britain, Iroquois Confederacy accomplishes separation of 13 British Colonies from Iroquois and Algonquin territory.

1785-91: migration northward of Seneca, Erie, Monsee, Oneida, Onondaga, and Cayuga, otherwise known as 'United Empire Loyalists.'

1797: Abitibi mother invents pea soup. Groundwork laid for Jehanne Benoit.

1812-1814: with heroic action against United States in northern New York and at 'Quebec,' Iroquois and Algonquin reinforce their covert power in Quebec society.

1837: disguised as the descendants of French farmers, Oddawa, Timiscami, Abitbi, and Saulteaux join Iroquois in attempted armed takeover of Power Corporation and Family Compact. Defeated, they hire Lord Durham, an unemployed theorist of noble savagery, to blame attempt on 'a people without a history.' Groundwork laid for present text.

1867: Iroquois leader Georges-Etienne Cartier secures integrity of Quebec within a new Canadian federation.

1873: Chicoutimi band teaches guestworkers aboriginal game 'hockey.'

1885: temporary setback as Louis Riel's execution is abetted by Paris-trained clergy.

1899: underground Algonquin chief Wilfrid Laurier sends 1000 white oppressors to die in Boer War.

1914-18: World War I distracts anglophone-Canadians from progress of aboriginal 'revenge of the cradle.'

1920-40: phenomenon known in aboriginal French literature as 'roman du terroir,' as more and more tribes adopt agricultural lifestyles.

1930: many Iroquois and Algonquin emigrate south to Abenaki and Massachussetts territory to seek employment. Groundwork laid for revival of U.S. fiction.

1936: aboriginal alliance invents 'Union Nationale' and brings about surprise election of Maurice Duplessis. First step in new program to disgust English-Canadians with Quebec.

1937: Iroquois elders secretly encourage 'Padlock Law.'

1937: Pipmauken band member invents snowmobile.

1944: Iroquois and their guestworkers return Duplessis to office, engineer 'Conscription Crisis.'

1948: Montagnais artist issues 'refus global.'

1949: Cree-Algonquin consortium acquires Johns-Manville company. Misunderstanding leads Duplessis government to send police to beat Thetford Mines workers. Groundwork laid for Barnabé case.

1957: Aboriginal alliance hires Saskatoon actor to play role 'Réal Caouette.'

1958: blond Saulteaux writer wins Prix France-Canada.

1962: Outimagami band begins payments to guestworker leader René Levesque who agrees to derail 'Quiet Revolution.'

1964: Missiquoi businessman writes song 'Jean le payeur.'

1969: Montréal, small guestworker community between Hochelaga and Oka, acquires Yankee baseball team. Mercenary hired to design stadium.

1970: renegade guestworker elements launch plot to expose

tribal alliances, torturing and scalping Kahnestake operative and kidnapping emissary of Great White Mother. With assistance of sympathetic Cubans, aboriginal alliances concealed.

1975: Cree offer homes to Vietnam refugees.

1976: many Iroquois and Algonquin move temporarily to Toronto, known in English as 'place of meeting,' to protect investments. Groundwork laid for Toronto restaurant boom.

1977: visiting French politico bribed to declare 'Vive le Mohawk libre.'

1978: aboriginal alliance invents 'Jacques Parizeau.' Hires younger brother of Robertson Davies to play role.

1980: failure of first referendum to establish aboriginal independence.

1982: first Algonquin lessons offered to Caribbean immigrants.

1985: Mohawk-Algonquin medical aid arrives in Eritrea.

1987: James Bay Cree purchase 'Hydro Québec' corporation to improve tribal fishstocks.

1992: Oka, major industrial city near Hochelaga, becomes site of guestworker unrest.

1993: guestworker activist Robert Bourassa fined for distributing illegal weapons at Oka.

1994: Kipawa memberships awarded to Neil Bissoondath, Pauline Julien, and Marco Micone for work toward cultural pluralism.

1995: in savage attack on wealth and non-guestworkers, 'Jacques Parizeau' galvanizes support for aboriginal sovereignty.

1997: secret Iroquois fund helps 'Jacques Parizeau' return from political exile. Referendum brings surprise recognition of Mathew Coon Come's government.

1998: 'safe zones' established at Deux-Montagnes and Schefferville for guestworkers and travellers.

1999: Mordecai Richler made honorary Inuit.

2006: Quebec mayor Ron ('Lasagne') Cross opens Winter Olympics.

2009: Hydro Québec acquires Disney in hostile takeover. Groundwork laid for liberation of what was once known in English as 'English Canada.'

Multiple Choice Games for Hiroshima Day

1. Hiroshima memory:
a) When I was five, I thought a 'hiroshima' was a plane.
b) When I was five, I thought a 'hiroshima' was the chrysanthemum on Japanese stamps.
c) When I was five, I pointed to a picture of the mushroom cloud. 'What is that?' I asked. 'That,' said my mother, 'is Hiroshima.'

2. Hiroshima history:
a) Hiroshima was the gateway to Itaku-Shima, the beautiful 'island of light.'
b) Hiroshima was the site of a haunting summer festival.
c) Hiroshima was an important military centre.

3. Hiroshima a-bomb triggers:

a) Suicidal Japanese soldiers caused the a-bombing of Hiroshima.

b) Dedicated American scientists caused the a-bombing of Hiroshima.

c) Patriotic American accountants caused the a-bombing of Hiroshima.

4. Hiroshima and good people:

a) A good person deplores radiation sickness.

b) A good person deplores killing anywhere.

c) A good person deplores having had to kill Huns, Nips, Nazis, skinheads, government agents, house invaders anywhere.

5. Hiroshima and Dresden:

a) What is different about Hiroshima and Dresden is that Dresden could be seen to resemble Coventry.

b) What is different about Hiroshima and Dresden is that there had been fewer Jews in Hiroshima.

c) What is different about Hiroshima and Dresden is that Germany didn't surrender ten days after.

6. Hiroshima and desperation:

a) During World War II more Japanese soldiers suicided than were captured by the U.S. Army.

b) During World War II more Japanese soldiers were captured than Japanese sailors were captured.

c) When a warship is sinking it is sometimes difficult to tell whether the sailors are suiciding or drowning.

7. Hiroshima and optimism:
a) The good thing about the Hiroshima bomb was that it taught children everywhere to make paper cranes.
b) The good thing about the Hiroshima bomb was that it taught North Americans that individual humans might live somewhere like Hiroshima.
c) The good thing about the Hiroshima bomb was that it made world leaders think about the third world war and forget the second.

8. To establish justification for the bombing of Hiroshima:
a) Ask a crewmember of the 'Enola Gay.'
b) Ask a scientist from the Manhattan project.
c) Ask a CNN columnist.
d) Ask a spokesperson for the Smithsonian.

138

9. Hiroshima and reporters:

a) Reports say the Japanese government was ready to surrender.

b) Reports say the Japanese armed forces would have never surrendered.

c) 'Reports' can also mean gunshots or a distant bomb blasts.

10. Hiroshima and consequences:

a) The Hiroshima bomb wiped out family life at the Shinomura Clock Factory.

b) The Hiroshima bomb wiped out the godliness of Japanese emperors.

c) The Hiroshima bomb wiped out Professor Suzuki's Japanese a-bomb program.

d) The Hiroshima bomb wiped out a herd of sheep in Mountain Springs Utah.

11. Hiroshima and power:

a) When the Hiroshima bomb was dropped Japan had 3.5 million soldiers on duty.

b) When the Hiroshima bomb was dropped, Japanese troops controlled all of Borneo, most of China, all of Korea, most of Thailand, all of Malaya, all of Viet Nam.

c) When the Hiroshima bomb was dropped there were three hundred and ninety thousand civilians in Japanese internment camps.

d) When the Hiroshima bomb was dropped, a Japanese-Canadian spacecraft could be observed observing at a safe distance.

12. Hiroshima and good things:

a) the good thing about the Hiroshima bomb is that it helped ordinary Japanese people not feel guilty about comfort women or medical experiments on Chinese prisoners.

b) the good thing about the Hiroshima bomb is that it helped humanity enjoy 50 years without fighting and killing.

c) the good thing about the Hiroshima bomb is that it helped Americans feel guilty about being winners.

13. Hiroshima and Canada:
a) Canadians and Belgians supplied uranium for the a-bomb and this makes them immoral.
b) Canadians and Belgians supplied uranium for the a-bomb but trusted the United States to act morally because they had studied United States history.
c) Canadians and Belgians should not have supplied uranium for the a-bomb because they had read *Huckleberry Finn.*
d) Canadians and Belgians supplied uranium for the a-bomb because they shared certain public policies with the United States and Japan on the treatment of other races.

14. Hiroshima and technology:

a) The people who died in the bombing of Tokyo are just as dead as those who died in Hiroshima.

b) The people who died at Nanking are just as dead as those who died in the bombing of Tokyo.

c) The people who died at Auschwitz are just as dead as those who died at Hiroshima.

d) The people who died at Hiroshima are just as dead as those who died at Guernica.

15. Hiroshima and love:

a) The best thing about the Hiroshima bomb is that it brought the Japanese and American people together.

b) The best thing about the Hiroshima bomb is that, although long exploded, it is still here.

c) The best thing about the Hiroshima bomb is *Hiroshima mon amour.*

16. Hiroshima and you:
a) When I was five, I thought wars were fought by soldiers.
b) When I was five, I thought tanks, bombers, and battleships were beautiful.
c) When I was five, I thought black-out curtains were a part of B.C. architecture.
d) When I was five, I thought the end of a war was a good thing.

Versions of some of these texts appeared previously in *Rampike, West Coast Line, The Dane Informer,* and *Paragraph.*

Front cover image is a detail from a Yugolavian war memorial now located in Slovenia. Photo by Frank Davey.